# LEFT IS RIGHT:

## *The Survival Guide For Living Lefty In A Right-Handed World*

### *by* **RAE LINDSAY**

GILMOUR  HOUSE

Englewood Cliffs, New Jersey

Published by GILMOUR HOUSE
Division of R & R Writers/Agents, Inc., 364 Mauro Road
Englewood Cliffs, New Jersey 07632
201-567-8986

Library of Congress Catalogue Card Number: 96-94650
ISBN: 0-965-37530-7

First Edition
Printed in the United States of America

*Graphics/Text Design: Gail Lee*
*Cover Design: Emily McGilvray*

## Dedication:

For my sister Camey,
always supportive,
always there for me.
I love her
dearly...even though
she's right-handed.

# Table of Contents:

*"The King fed himself
with his left hand,
as did we."*

James Boswell,
The Life of Johnson,
1791

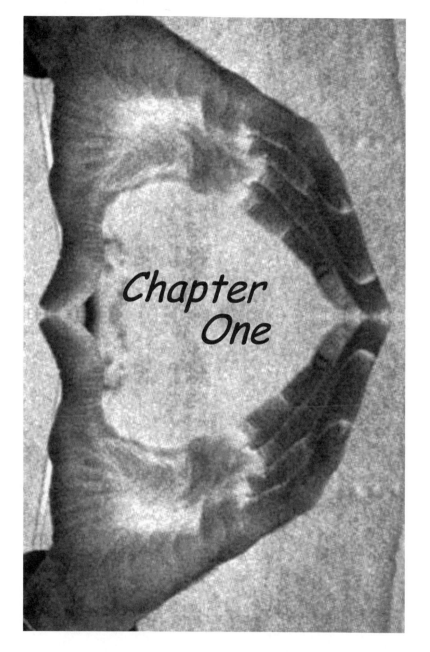

Chapter
One

# LEFTIES UNITE!

What do *Bill Clinton, Jay Leno, Monica Seles, Bruce Willis, Jerry Seinfeld, Paul McCartney, Pablo Picasso, Oprah Winfrey,* and *Napoleon* have in common?

If you answer "they are all left-handed," *right on,* because these famous men and women are among the thousands of left-handers who have left their mark on the world. Left-handed people are special because we are different. If Clinton and the celebrated coterie cited above had been born right-handed, they might never have achieved the fame history has awarded them.

Look around you. Most of your friends, maybe your parents and the rest of the family are right-handed. Right-handed people have the world going in their direction. We drive our cars on the right side of the road; when we play baseball, the bases go from right to left; and we paste postage stamps on the right side of the envelope. We dial a telephone with our right hand, take a picture using our right forefinger to click the shutter, turn a doorknob to the right to open a door. We read books and write letters from left to right, because that's how books are printed and the way we've been taught to write.

But that wasn't always the case. There was a time, centuries ago, when both hands were equally important, when tools were used with either hand and writing went from *right to left*. Later on we'll tell you why and when this direction changed.

As it is with so many things in life, though, the majority wins, and the majority of people in this world are right-handed. We lefties, however, are not such a small minority. One researcher, Dr. Bryng Bryngelson of the University of Minnesota, who spent thirty years studying left-handers, estimated that thirty-five out of every one hundred children born in the world would be lefties if parents or teachers or social customs didn't force them to switch. (And, his research showed that an additional 3 percent would use either hand with equal dexterity).

Even with millions of switchovers, in the United States the actual left-handed population is about 40 million. This figure, representing roughly 15 percent of the population, creeps upward every year, not because more left-handed children are born, but because fewer lefties are being switched or trained to use their right hands. On a worldwide basis, it is estimated that as many as 200 to 250 million people were born with a disposition towards left-handedness. (That's almost the total population of the United States.)

In technical terms, lefties are referred to as *sinistrals* (from the Latin, meaning "on the left"), right-handers are called *destrals* (Latin for "on the right"), and people who perform some tasks with one hand and some with the other, or the same tasks with *either* hand are called *ambidextrals* or *ambidextrous*. This is a confusing misnomer, however, because "ambidextrous" literally means "having *two* right hands."

As we progressed from the primitive life of the cave dwellers to the rich cultures and contributions of ancient Greece and Rome and into what we know as modern times, the gap between left and right became wider and wider. In fact, not only was left or right attributed to handedness, but also to geographic location: some object or place on the right side, or the left side. Superstitions, traditions, and religious customs became associated with the left side or the right side. These ranged from close attention to the direction the sun moves (from left to right if you're facing south) to the famous left-handed handshake of Boy Scouts all over the world.

In the following chapters, we'll report on these traditions and customs...we'll tell you about some of the famous people in history who have been left-handed, either naturally or because of accidents to their right hands...and we will talk about the everyday things that cause most left-handers to think or act ambidextrously-things as simple as using a scissors or turning the pages of this book.

Half a century ago, a left-handed child grew up learning to do dozens of ordinary tasks with the right hand–because either this was the way he or she was taught, or it was the way most machines and tools worked. I, for example, learned how to bat as a righty, and still knit right-handed. Today in the United States, lefties are much more widely accepted, and special appliances and tools have been designed just for us. There are even a handful of enterprising stores across the country and throughout the world that specialize in dozens of left-handed items.

The famous Scottish historian, *Thomas Carlyle,* who became left-handed by default, as it were, after a serious injury to his right hand, said right-handedness is "the very oldest institution that exists." Carlyle lived more than one hundred years ago (1795 to 1881). He would be pleased to see that now, on the eve of the millenium, lefties have gained their own rights and a good bit of recognition and have made a solid dent in that centuries-old institution.

###

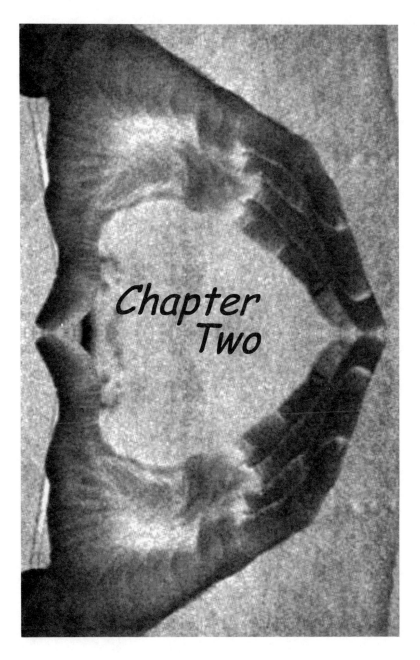

Chapter
Two

# Welcome To The Club!

While right-handed people rarely think about which hand another person is using, lefties are quick to spot a fellow southpaw. We've been watching other members of our exclusive club since the beginning of recorded history.

And why not? The ranks of sensational sinistrals runs the gamut from *Alexander the Great* to *Bill Clinton,* the 42nd President; from Renaissance man *Michelangelo* to modern master, *Pablo Picasso*; from undersized *David,* who brought down Goliath with a sling shot to the overwhelming linebacker *William "The Refrigerator" Perry;* from creative businessmen like *Benjamin Franklin* to financial wizard *H. Ross Perot*; from horizontally-challenged *Napoleon* to standing-in-the-wings *Prince William* of England. Lefty luminaries include *Albert Einstein* and *Bill Gates*, who might–or might not–have enjoyed swapping trade secrets. *Jay Leno* rules the late night TV stage, while *Charlie Chaplin* was the king of silent cinema.

Let's not forget the ladies: *Napoleon's* wife, *Josephine,* surely wielded some left-handed influence and her own chapter in history books, while O.J. Simpson prosecutor *Marcia Clark* made headlines during the "trial of the century" and then wrote a best-selling book about

*Napoleon Bonaparte rode into the Battle of Wagram in Austria with a telescope held firmly in his left hand, to survey the scene with his left eye.*

her adventure.

There are also more than a few sinister sinestral skeletons in the left-door closet, including England's *Jack the Ripper* and our very own American *Billy the Kid.*

Here are some legendary lefties, past and present, men and women who changed the world, from history-makers to record-breakers, from the global scene to the tv screen.

# WORLD LEADERS

Although lefties have been around since—we think—Adam and Eve, the first mega left-handed leader dates back to the fourth century B.C. when *Alexander the Great* (356-323 B.C.) of Macedonia conquered the Persian Empire. A few centuries later, *Julius Caesar* (102-44 B.C.) ruled over the entire Roman Empire. Even though he was left-handed, he favored the right-handed hand-shake and insisted it be used throughout the Empire. By then it was widely believed that anything associated with "right" meant "good," while "left" was considered a bad omen.

Another left-handed world leader was *Napoleon,* who was often shown in portraits with his left arm placed slightly behind his back at the waist, a convenient position for drawing his sword. Some historians credit Napoleon with the practice of driving on the left side of the road, still the only way to go in Britain and some of its former dominions. Napoleon's rationale? He thought drivers of military transports were safer on the left

*Long-reigning Queen Victoria passed on the left-handed scepter to her grandson, King George VI, and his grandson, PrinceCharles, current heir to the English throne, and Charles' son, Prince William, number one in line to succeed his father when Charles becomes King.*

because the foliage and trees that lined the left side of the road provided some protection from attack. On the left side, too, they could use their sword-bearing right arms to fight any intruders who came from the right. His left-handed "better half," *Josephine*, made no known military pronouncements or decisions, but her influence made history from Russia (where he lost the battle) to Elba (where he lost his life).

*Joan of Arc* also fought for France, but in her case she won the battle but lost her life when she was sold to the English she had fought against, and it was only after her death in 1431 that she became a symbol of heroic patriotism. Our own retired General *Norman Schwarzkopf,* on the other hand, is a hero in his own time, celebrated for his triumphs in the Persian Gulf War against Iraq.

England has had its own share of left-handed leaders–and rulers–past and present, including *George II,* king from 1727 to 1760, whose tax rates and long-distance governing eventually led to the American Revolution, and *Queen Victoria,* who reigned from 1837 to 1901. Although being left-handed was not the favored choice in Victorian days, Victoria's great-great grandson *Prince Charles,* the present heir to the throne, was never discouraged from favoring his left hand. Ironically, Charles' grandfather, *King George VI,* Queen Elizabeth's father, was a switched leftie who, not untypically, stuttered badly. Many of the broadcast speeches he recorded from the time he took over for his abdicating brother the Duke of Windsor, until the time he died, had to be heavily edited. Today, young *Wills, aka The Prince of Wales,* wields his wicket bat, while not yet the scepter, with his left hand.

In the United States, we have a rather long list of left-handed leaders, dating back to *Benjamin Franklin*, who never quite made it to the White House. The ill-fated *James A. Garfield's* term as twentieth president was aborted by his assassination in 1881. But the twentieth century has seen a richness of lefties in the highest office and next in line, beginning with *Harry Truman*, thirty-third president (1945-1953), and then *Gerald Ford*, thirty-eighth president (1974-1977), and Ford's vice-president, *Nelson Rockefeller*. In fact, three of the last five presidents have been southpaws: Ford, then number 41, *George Bush*, and currently, *Bill Clinton*. In 1992, all three presidential wannabes, including Clinton, *Perot*, and then-pres Bush were left-handed; in 1996, we had another sinistral triumverate of contenders: Clinton, Perot, and former Senator *Bob Dole*, who became a lefty as a result of injuries to his right hand suffered in World War II.

# PUBLIC FIGURES

*Benjamin Franklin*, that talented inventor, writer, and statesman, believed that being left-handed was a disadvantage in a right-handed world. In an essay called "The Left Hand," he wrote:

> *I address myself to all my friends of youth, and conjure them to direct their compassionate regards to my unhappy fate, in order to remove the prejudices of which I am the victim...if by chance I touched a pencil, a pen, or a needle, I was... rebuked; and more than once I have been beaten for being awkward, and wanting a graceful manner.*

*In 1994 President Clinton strongly emphasizes a
point with his left hand.*

Still, Franklin effectively used his left hand to tie the kite in his pioneering study on electricity. He was also the only man to have signed (with his left hand, of course) all four papers relating to the founding of the United States: the Declaration of Independence, the Treaty of Alliance with France, the Treaty of Paris (which ended the Revolutionary War), and the U.S. Constitution.

Another famous left-handed American was *Albert Einstein*, the Nobel prize-winning physicist and mathematician who modestly declared he only had "two good ideas" in his entire life, one of which was the theory of relativity. Although he has not gone on record for the number of good ideas he has had, *Bill Gates*, currently the CEO of Microsoft, certainly had a winner in his Windows software, installed on millions of computers the world over. In 1996, *Time* listed Gates as Number 2 on its list of the "10 Most Powerful Men in America," preceded only by that other powerful southpaw, President *Bill Clinton.*

*Gates*, who is moving into many new cyberworld venues (including MSNBC, and *Slate*, a magazine on the World Wide Web) has been cited as the World's richest private citizen with an $18 billion dollar fortune, and has far outpaced another computer wizard who parlayed a good idea into billions of bucks: *H. Ross Perot,* whose Electronic Data Systems (E.D.S., a computerized business systems implementation) gave him the resources to spend over $60 million on his '92 bid for the Presidency. *Steve Forbes* also spent his own millions in the 1996 Republican primaries (throwing a left-handed punch into the plans of Dole, Buchanan et al). But Forbes' bankroll, unlike Perot's self-made millions, came from his grandfather and flamboyant father, Malcolm S.

Forbes, who built the tremendously successful publishing empire of which *Forbes* magazine is the influential cornerstone.

# COMPOSERS, MUSICIANS

There are few left-handed classical musicians and composers who achieved any degree of fame, possibly because their left-handedness made it difficult to play any instrument engineered for right-handers, except, of course, the piano or organ, or the "two-handed" sax, clarinet, trombone, etc. One who found his sinistral niche in the music world was *Carl Philipp Emanuel Bach*, the son of Johann Sebastican Bach. Carl was more famous than his father during his own lifetime. Another classical composer, although right-handed, is a hero to lefties: *Maurice Ravel*, best known for *Bolero and Scheherazade*, wrote a special concerto for the left hand in honor of a pianist friend who had lost his right hand in World War I. One of America's unique contributors to music well-loved and well-sung the world over is *Cole Porter*, who wrote emotionally, humorously, joyfully, and sadly about LOVE, in such songs as *Begin the Beguine, I Get A Kick Out of You, I Love Paris, It's Delovely, Anything Goes,* and *Night and Day*.

Among contemporary musicians, the folk-rock star *Bob Dylan* is left-handed, and so was *Jimi Hendrix* and fifty percent of the former Beatles, *Paul McCartney* and *Ringo Starr*. Other popular musicians are *Paul Simon, Melissa Manchester,* and *Phil Collins*. Still on the scene today–although his popularity waned decades ago–is the unique *Tiptoe Through The Tulips* enforcer, *Tiny Tim*.

*Paul McCartney plays lefty during the Beatles' first trip to Germany in 1960, wh*
*there were still* **five Beatles**, *an unknown group of musicians from Liverpool*

Astrid

# ARTISTS

*Leonardo da Vinci* (1452-1519) was the creative Italian genius who painted (most notably, "The Mona Lisa"), sculpted, and dreamed up dozens of inventions and ingenious designs ranging from an airplane, a helicopter, and a submarine, to an alarm clock, an oil lamp and skin-diving equipment–almost five hundred years ago! *Leonardo* was fanatically secretive about his projects: he wrote all his notes from right to left, enabling them to be deciphered only by using a mirror. He, however, was able to read and write in this reverse way *without* a mirror.

　　*Leonardo* meant so much to the history of the city of Rome that not only is its airport named after him, but a huge statue of him dominates the scene–he welcomes visitors with a wave of his *left hand.*

　　An Italian contemporary of *Leonardo's* was *Michelangelo* (1475-1564), whose renowned works include the massive Sistine Chapel at the Vatican, a task which took more than four years to complete. Michelangelo was so versatile he taught himself to use either hand to paint so he could switch when one hand became cramped. Good thing, too, or it would have taken more than eight years to finish the job!

　　Two other famous left-handed artists of the Renaissance period were also known for their religious paintings. During *Raphael's* short life (1483-1520) he created many beautiful madonnas (*Sistine Madonna, Madonna of the Meadow*), while *Hans Holbein* (1497-1543), also immortalized royalty in *Jane Seymour* and *Christina of Denmark.*

*"Girl Before a Mirror"*, one of Pablo Picasso's many dual image paintings; here the artist's subject prominently points her **left hand.**

In our own century, *Pablo Picasso* (1881- 1973) led the ranks of left-handed artists, although *Paul Klee* (1879-1940), commands his own place in the development of what is known as "modern art." Those who are not aficionados of Picasso's abstract view of his subjects might be inclined to think that, in his case, "the right hand didn't know what the left hand was doing."

# WRITERS

As noted, it may be difficult for southpaws to write *legibly*, but that never stopped them from writing *creatively*. Among the most creative, *James Michener*, whose many memorable novels include *Tales of the South Pacific*, *Hawaii*, and *The Bridges of Toko-ri*; and *H.G. Wells*, author of *The Time Machine*, and dozens of other fiction and non-fiction books. Wells envisioned a world of the future, and *Lewis Carroll* created a world through a looking glass, which we talk about later, but *Peter Benchley* has always been fascinated by the world underwater, and wrote about it in *Jaws*, and *The Deep*.

# ENTERTAINERS

Show biz in all its forms is well represented by lefties. Among comics were *W.C. Fields* and one of the famous Marx brothers, *Harpo*, who played the harp with his left hand. Another frustrated musician who became one of the most famous comic stars of all time was *Charlie Chaplin*, whose career as a violinist was aborted by the problem of reversing the strings on a violin to accommodate his left-handedness. Even had he perse-vered, imagine the awkwardness of one left-handed vio-linist among a sea of orchestra righties. Famous mime, *Marcel Marceau*, made his audiences laugh without say-ing a word.

*Danny Kaye* was a much-praised all-around enter-tainer who appeared in many classic film roles. He was Papa Gepetto in *Pinocchio*, working his puppets with his left hand, and Captain Hook in *Peter Pan*, where he wielded his sword southpaw-style. More recently, *Dick Van Dyke* played similar roles, notably in *Mary Poppins*, and *Chitty, Chitty Bang, Bang*, as well as foil to Mary Tyler Moore in the long-running *Dick Van Dyke Show* (1961-1966).

Other contemporary comic lefties include two on the *Seinfeld* team, *Jerry Seinfeld* and *Jason Alexander; Tim Allen* of TV's *Home Improvements* and such films as *The Santa Clause; Alan Thicke* of *Growing Pains;* and *Eddie Albert* of the long-running *Green Acres.* Holding court in non-sit-com venues are eternally nasty funnyman *Don Rickels*, eternally smiling exercise ma-ven *Richard Simmons*, and TV late night king *Jay Leno* (who outdraws that more serious southpaw commenta-tor, *Ted Koppel*). *Allen Funt* made us laugh at our own antics on *Candid Camera*, and *Wink Martindale* was m.c. of more game shows than anyone in history– *Trivial Pur-suit, Wheel of Fortune, Tic Tac Dough, Joker's Wild, and Debt.* A left-handed genius who undeniably shaped the lives of any American youngsters close to a tv set in the last half of this century (which counts almost ev-eryone) was *Jim Henson*, creater of all the muppets and the fabulous Miss Piggie.

The distaff side has their fair share of  leave-

'em-laughing lefties, too. Comediennes/actresses include *Cloris Leachman, Goldie Hawn, Whoopie Goldberg,* and *Fran Drescher.* One left-handed lady who can make you laugh...and cry...is *Oprah Winfrey,* who interestingly named her company Harpo Productions which is not only Oprah spelled backwards, but also commemorates the great southpaw comic.

The list of left-handed leading men in films, theater and TV includes that all-time charmer, *Cary Grant* (*An Affair to Remember,* ); *Robert Redford,* noted for *The Sting, The Way We Were,* ; *Rock Hudson,* (*Giant, Pillow Talk*); *Michael Crawford* (Broadway's Phantom of the Opera) and *Michael Landon,* director and star of TV's *Little House on the Prairie.* Among the ranks of heavy action stars are *Rocky's Sylvester Stallone, Diehard's Bruce Willis, Speed's Keanu Reeves, The Great Escape's Steve McQueen, Easy Rider's Peter Fonda,* and *Paul Michael Glaser,* who shot left-handed as Starsky of the TV series, *Starsky and Hutch.*

As for lefty leading ladies, the list is headed by singer/actress *Judy Garland,* who will always be remembered as Dorothy in *The Wizard of Oz. Marilyn Monroe,* immortalized in 1994 with a portrait on a postage stamp, left her own unforgettable legacy in such films as *Seven Year Itch, Some Like It Hot,* and *The Misfits.* Another beautiful blonde was *Kim Novak,* who starred in *Picnic, Vertigo, The Man With the Golden Arm,* and *Moll Flanders,* in which she had to learn to fence with her left hand. *Cicily Tyson,* commemorated the trials of a former slave in *The Autobiography of Miss Jane Pitman* (for which she won an Emmy in 1973), while *Julia Roberts,* played another type of Southern woman in *Steel Magnolias,* before she became Richard Gere's *Pretty Woman.*

# SPORTS STARS

Although southpaws are more than respectfully represented in all major sports, some activities are really right
up a lefty's alley...yes, this includes bowling.

*Baseball:* Lefties really excel on the diamond.  Thirty-
two percent of all major league batters (half the batters
in the Hall of Fame are either left-handed or switch-hit-
ters), 30 percent of major league pitchers, and 48 percent of big league first basemen are left-handed–but there
are no major league left-handed catchers!

Left-handed first basemen are in such demand
because a common but difficult play involves a ground
ball hit to first base, so the first baseman has to throw
to second for the force play and be ready to receive
the ball back at first for a double play.  This causes
problems for a righty, who has to first catch the ball,
then *turn* his body toward second and throw–a movement which wastes time.  A lefty doesn't have to reverse his body position at all.

A right-handed pitcher's curve ball starts at the
outside of the plate and curves across the middle of it.
To a right-handed batter it seems as if the ball is going
to hit him and the batter will "bail out" (step away from
the plate), and have a strike called on him.  In this situation, a left-handed batter against a right-handed
pitcher is at an *advantage* because the ball curves *into*
his power, and if he connects he can hit a long ball.

The reverse could be true with left-handed pitchers against right-handed batters, but since most righties
only come up against left-handed pitchers maybe a third

*The Chicago Cubs batter's view of Los Angeles Dodger southpaw Sandy Koufax in 1962 as he established a National League record with 18 strikeouts in one game.*

of their times at bat, they are uncomfortable with the direction and curve of the pitch.

As for catchers, the problem for lefties in that position occurs when a runner is trying to steal second and the catcher has to be able to throw to second base quickly. Since most batters are right-handed, the left-handed catcher would have to move to the side before throwing, to avoid hitting the batter. Again, this takes precious time. But as more and more left-handed hitters begin to play ball, the handedness of the catcher will become less crucial. The famous Yankee catcher-then-manager *Yogi Berra* (who became almost as well known for his malapropisms as his athletic ability–"It ain't over till it's over") got around handily by catching right-handed, but *batting* as a lefty. (The "Bear" played in 10 world championships and 75 World Series games). Some of the most famous southpaw players include:

*Lou "The Iron Horse" Gehrig*, first baseman for the Yankees (who incidentally seemed to have had a preponderance of lefty super-stars), played 2,130 consecutive games before side-lined by illness, a record only broken in 1995 by the Baltimore Oriole's Cal Ripkin.

*Babe Ruth*, the unforgettable, unbeatable Babe, who held the record for life-time home runs (714 until Hank Aaron broke the record in 1974 with 715) and played in more World Series than any other player. Yankee Stadium ("The House That Ruth Built") favors southpaw sluggers since the shortened right field makes it easier for lefty batters to hit balls out of the park.

*Roger Maris*, the Yankee outfielder who broke another

*In Boston's Fenway Park, lefty Reggie Jackson takes a healthy swing on a strike in the sixth inning of a Red Sox-Yankee game in October, 1978. Later on, in the eighth inning, Jackson connected for a winning home run for the Yankees, making them the Eastern Division Champs.*

of Ruth's records by hitting 61 home runs on the last day of the 1961 season. For 30 years this record-breaker was disputed, since Maris played in 162 games, while Ruth hit his 60 homers in only 154 games, but in 1991 the baseball powers-that-be recognized Maris' achievement.

*Ty Cobb*, widely regarded as the greatest player in history and one of the first players elected to the Hall of Fame, batted lefty, but threw with his right hand.

*Whitey Ford*, ace pitcher for the Yankees during the fifties and sixties, holds the second best winning percentage in baseball history and 8 pitching records in World Series play (he pitched in 11 Series games and won 10).

*Reggie Jackson* played with the Yanks before joining the California Angels; he ranks sixth in all-time home runs and drove in over 100 runs in six different years.

*Ron Guidry*, another Yankees star pitcher, who won 20-plus games in three separate seasons.

*Don Mattingly*, a Yanks' star from 1982-1989, hit six grand slams in 1987.

*Sandy Koufax*, the "Man With the Golden Arm," a strike-out king who won twenty-seven games in one season for the Los Angeles Dodgers.

*Stan Musial* played in over three thousand games with a life-time .331 average and was National League batting champ seven times.

*Jim Abbott*, who was born without a right hand, was drafted by the Toronto Blue Jays and in 1987 won the Sullivan Award as an amateur athlete. He was the winning pitcher in the 1988 Olympics and then pitched for the Yankees. During his six-year career, through the 1994 season, he had a 65-74 record with 5 shutouts; he also struck out 693 batters.

What about women on the diamond? Although there are dozens of women's softball teams nationwide, there was only one brief period when women were officially recognized as hardball players–during World War II, when male major league players were off fighting for their country, a period dramatized in the film, *A League of Their Own*. Before that women played in "exhibition games." One of the stars of this circuit was pitcher *Jackie Mitchell* who, at age 17, in 1931, pitched against Babe Ruth and Lou Gehrig and *struck them both out!* The day after this feat, the baseball commissioner banished Mitchell from the game because it was "too strenuous for women." Nicknamed the "Chattanooga Southpaw," Mitchell continued to play for another seven years before she retired.

*Golf:* Left-handed golfers are at a distinct advantage when they golf *right-handed* because the left arm is really the power arm in the golf swing. So, while it might seem as if they are switching to their less powerful arm, this isn't true at all–these crafty golfers are really capitalizing on their left-handed strength. Another reason most lefties play golf right-handed is that left-handed clubs are very expensive for young golfers starting out. Among the top players in the last twenty-five years only *Bob Charles* actually golfs left-handed. Sam Adams, Ben Hogan, and *Johnny Miller* are all lefties who play right-handed.

*Tennis:* This is another great sport for lefties because it confuses right-handed players. A left-handed player is accustomed to playing against righties, but a right-handed opponent must reverse his or her techniques when up against a lefty, and this often proves unsettling. A righty, for example, has to serve to a different area of the court to place the ball to a lefty's backhand. Some famous, trophy-winning tennis southpaws include *Jimmy Conners, Rod Laver, Roscoe Tanner, Guillermo Vilas, Monica Seles, John McInroe, Thomas Muster, Martina Navratilova,* and *Renee Richards.*

*Football:* For running backs or defense players there is no advantage or disadvantage to being left-handed. However, a left-handed quarterback, such as former college star *Frankie Albert* or *Kenny Stabler* who played for the Oakland Raiders, offers the element of surprise to an unsuspecting opposition. Some recent stars include:

*William "The Refrigerator" Perry*, linebacker, the Chicago Bears; *Deion Sanders*, an all-purpose player, who brought the Super Bowl with him to two teams in two consecutive years (San Francisco 49'ers and Dallas Cowboys); *Boomer Esiason*, quarterback, New York Jets; *Steve Young*, quarterback, San Francisco 49'ers.

*Boxing:* Left-handed boxers make right-handed ones look awkward because the righties aren't used to deal-

*One of the famous lefty tennis players, Jimmy Conners returns the ball during a match in 1979. Conners cruised to a 6-1, 6-2 win in the Masters Grand Prix Tennis Championship.*

ing with punches coming from the reversed direction. Consequently, it's difficult for lefties to get fights–a situation portrayed so vividly in the *Rocky* movies by *Sylvester Stallone*, one of Hollywood's most visible left-handed action heroes. One lefty boxer in real-life who succeeded was *James J. "Gentleman Jim" Corbett,* heavyweight boxing champion from 1892 to 1897. Another was *Paul "The Astoria Assassin" Berlenbach*, so-called because of his devastating left hook which helped him win the light-heavyweight championship in 1925.

## *Bowling:* Athough only 15 percent of pro bowlers are lefties, they rake in about 60 percent of all the earnings. One reason is that thousands of games are bowled on each bowling alley and since more bowlers are right-handed, the alleys acquire miniscule "grooves" on one side. The bowler who is trying to control the ball often finds that it falls into one of these subtle grooves. But the side of the alley is really much "cleaner" for lefties, and they can control the ball more effectively. *Earl Anthony* is probably the best-known professional left-handed bowler...he won hundreds of thousands of dollars in tournaments before he retired in 1991, and still holds the record for 41 tournaments won during his career. Anthony wanted to be a left-handed pitcher, but an ankle injury led him to bowling instead. Other lefty bowling greats include *Mike McGarth, Marty Piraino, Fat Sam Trivett, and Roy Trivett.*

## *Miscellaneous Sports:* Bruce Jenner won the 1976 Olympic Decathlon; *Dorothy Hamill* won her gold medal for figure skating  in the 1976 Olympics, *Pele* helped

popularize soccer in America; *Mark Spitz* swam his way to 7 gold medals in the 1972 Summer Olympics; *Angel Cordero* rode dozens of thoroughbreds to victory, spurring them on with his left-hand-held crop; and *David Robinson*, one of a handful of southpaw hoop stars, played on the fabulous "Dream Team" during the 1986 Summer Olympics.

# LEGAL LEFTIES

The most famous American left-handed legal luminary of our century is *Clarence Darrow*, who defended John T. Scopes in the famous–or infamous, depending on your point of view–"Monkey Trial" in Dayton, Tennessee in 1925. Although Scopes was found guilty for defying a ban on teaching the man-is-descended-from-apes theory of evolution, Darrow scored heavily with his defense of free speech and scientific enlightenment. The Scopes trial generated headlines all over the world, but never came close to the media attention given to the "Trial of the Century," which starred O.J. Simpson. Another star was fiery *Marcia Clark*, one of the Los Angeles prosecutors who went mano-a-mano against Simpson's "Dream Team" of defenders including southpaw *F. Lee Bailey*. Although Clark was paid millions for her book about the trial, Supreme Court Justice *Ruth Bader-Ginsberg* will probably never make millions from her tales on the bench, but this left-handed litigator's contributions to the American judicial system will far outlast the fame of Bailey and Clark. Earning a million or more was not the goal of attorney *Caroline Kennedy Schlossberg*, the daughter of President Kennedy, in writing her books (including a recent treatise on "privacy"). Instead her aim was to protect the rights of individuals, a goal her Attorney General uncle, Robert, and many Kennedy cousins seem to have in common.

## NOT-SO-LEGAL LEFTIES

Unfortunately, we do have our sinister exceptions including such notorious notables as *John Dillinger*, who robbed banks and killed at least 16 people in 1933, which earned him the title of "Public Enemy Number One." There is also *William H. Bonney, Billy the Kid*, the Wild West killer who was actually born in New York, and murdered 21 people before he died at age 21 in 1880. A terror in our own time was *The Boston Strangler, Albert Henry de Salvo*, who was accused of 300 rapes and assaults and confessed to 13 murders between June, 1962 and January, 1964. De Salvo was defended, incidentally, by that lefty lawyer of O.J. fame, *F. Lee Bailey.*

But murderous villainy is not restricted to this side of the Atlantic, as demonstrated by England's infamous *Jack the Ripper*, who was accused of murdering 14 young women, beginning in 1888. After studying each victim, investigators realized the "modus operandi" was similar for every murder: Jack the Ripper would grab his victim from behind, hold her with his right arm, and then use his left hand to slit her throat from right to left. A right-handed person would have cut in the opposite way—from left to right. It was rumoured that *Queen Victoria's* left-handed grandson, the *Duke of Clarence*, who was thought to be insane because of venereal disease, was "the ripper," but this was never proven and no one was ever tried for the murders.

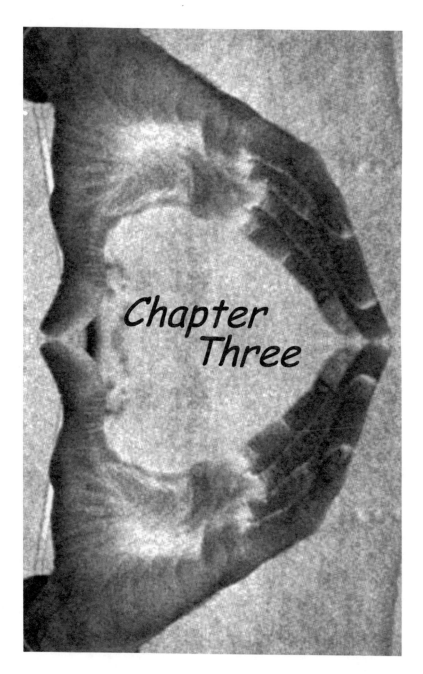

Chapter
Three

# Did You Ever See A Left-Handed Caveman?

In the early dawn of civilization, all men and women used whichever hand was most convenient for finding food, climbing hills and mountains, building shelters, and even drawing pictures on the walls of their caves.

Most anthropologists agree that handedness was probably split evenly between lefties and righties thousands of years ago. Artifacts found all over the world prove that Stone Age man (2,000,000-8000 B.C.) made crude instruments which could be used with either hand. Flints, arrowheads, early knives or carving implements were made with double-beveling–sharpened edges on both sides–for use with either hand. By the time of the Bronze Age (3500-600 B.C.), however, as tools became more sophisticated, they required hand specialization. And more often than not, the tools that were developed were right-handed ones.

Such tools became prized possessions to be passed on from generation to generation. So, if a man made a tool to be used in the right hand, his children and grandchildren were taught to use that tool with the right hand, whether they had a tendency to be left-handed or not.

As an example, the first sickle for cutting grain or edible grasses was developed in the Bronze Age. It was designed to be used with the right hand, and to this day there is no such thing as a sickle for use with the left hand. Clearly, almost by default, as people became more and more civilized, the right hand became the "right" hand to use with tools, in customs, and even in language.

The alphabet, however, was a different story. The first alphabet read from right-to-left and was invented by the Phoenicians, a Mediterranean seafaring tribe which thrived around 3000 to 2000 B.C. As sailors and explorers, they introduced their right-to-left writing to Egypt and Greece. All samples of writing that date back earlier than 600 B.C. move in this right-to-left direction which we know now as "mirror-writing." Here's an example:

tfeL oT thgiR morF etorW snaicineohP ehT

By about the fifth century B.C., the Greeks began to write from left-to-right, mainly because of the increasing number of customs and superstitions associated with going in the "right" direction (from left-to-right). Arab and other Semitic nations, however, continued to read and write from right-to-left, as they do today. Modern Hebrew and Arabic are only two of several languages referred to as "left-handed tongues." One theory for why these left-handed tongues continue in use is that they are rooted in religious literature (such as the Bible and Koran) and followers believe it would be sacrilegious to distort or change them in any way.

The ancient Greeks tried to explain handedness and why the right hand should be more dominant. One theory they advanced was related to the body's center of gravity. They felt that since the liver and lungs were on the right side of the body–they didn't realize we have a *pair* of lungs–people were able to balance better on their left foot. This kept the right hand free for action. In time, they reasoned, the muscles on the right foot and right hand developed more strongly.

Another early theory was that men carried their shields in their left hands to protect the heart. This made their right hands, which carried weapons, stronger. But nobody ever explained how this applied to women, who never carried weapons or shields.

Whatever the theories, by the time the Bible was being written, the right hand was clearly the more important, *good* hand. In the Bible there are more than a hundred positive mentions of the right hand but very few credits for the left. Eve, for example, was created out of Adam's *left* rib, and throughout history, women have been trying to overcome that weak identification and achieve status as equals.

In the New Testament, when Matthew mentions the second coming of the Lord, he says,

> *He shall separate them one from another, as a shepherd divideth his sheep from the goats and he shall set the sheep on his right hand, but the goats on his left. Then shall the King say unto them on his right hand* (the sheep), *Come, ye blessed of my Father, inherit the Kingdom prepared from the foundations of the world.*

There was one group of lefties described in the Old Testament who became notorious. Ironically, they were members of the tribe of Benjamin (*Ben Yamin* literally means "Son of the Right Hand") and were called the "Seven Hundred Slingers," warriors who used slingshots in their left hands. These seven hundred "could sling stones at an hair breadth, and not miss." Their claim to fame was one of terror and warfare, but at the same time, they were described in the Bible as men of courage and valor. Interestingly, a contemporary Israeli of courage and valor, Prime Minister *Binyamin Netanyahu,* is left handed!

By the time of the Roman Empire (27 B.C.-A.D. 1453), right was "right" and left was often left out. Julius Caesar, arguably the most famous Roman emperor, was left-handed himself, but he decreed that the alphabet would henceforth go from left to right, and that the formal way to greet another Roman was with a right-handed shake.

By now "left-handed" or "left-sided" and "right-handed" and "right-sided" began to take on very special meanings.

### ###

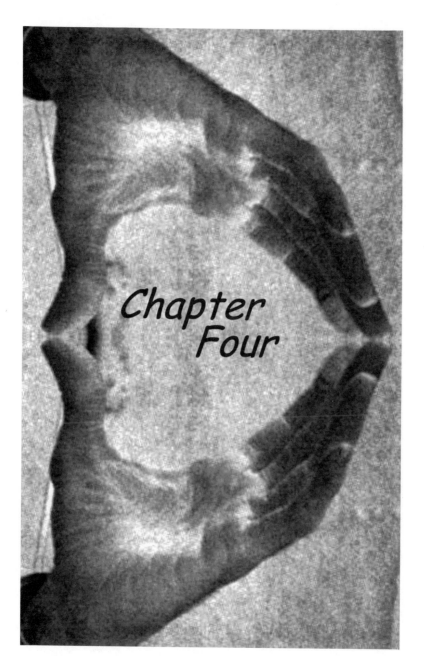

Chapter
Four

# Why Are Some Of Us Left-Handed?

Aside from superstitions and traditions about handedness, scientists, doctors, and even philosophers have for centuries been trying to explain why some people are left-handed and others right-handed.

Almost 2,500 years ago, the famous Greek philosopher, Plato, believed that the hand that rocks the baby rules which hand the baby will favor. Say for example, that a baby is always held in its mother's left arm so that the right-handed mother can give the baby a bottle with her right hand. The child will begin to use its own left arm because the right one is tucked next to the mother's body. Since Plato theorized this would make most children in the world *left-handed*, he urged mothers to feed and rock their babies holding them in their right arms.

Another theory is based on the idea that we *inherit* the tendency to be left-handed. But this is refuted by the fact that 80 percent of left-handed children are born to right-handed parents. As further proof that the heredity theory doesn't hold up, only one of the famous Dionne quintuplets, born in Canada in 1934, *Marie*, was left-handed.

Toward the end of the nineteenth century, another early investigator of the left-handed phenomenon, Sir Cyril Burt, found that in 75 percent of the population the bones of the right arm are longer and stronger, but in 9 percent of the population, the left arm is longer and stronger. (The arm strength/length of the remaining 16 percent is never revealed). But further tests showed that at the time of birth, the length of both arms in all babies is identical. The conclusion has to be that the bones and muscles in the "preferred hand"– the hand we use for most things as we grow up–will be better developed by use and skill, not because of birth.

Since 1900 there have been other explanations for handedness: some people believed that it is related to the rotation of the sun. Others maintained that left-handed children are rebellious and simply insist on using the opposite (left) hand. Still others thought that left-handedness was the result of brain damage.

## THE ANSWER LIES IN THE BRAIN

Initially, when scientists turned to the brain to solve the mystery of hand-preference, they believed that left-handedness was a genetic situation which produces the exact reverse effects of being right-handed. But this theory was refuted by *Dr. Jeannine Herron* of the University of California, and herself a lefty, who explained, "Left-handedness is not a mirror of right-handedness. Left-handers differ in at least two particular ways: they use their non-preferred hand much more often, and may have a different brain organization."

According to *Dr. Herron,* we don't have one beautifully symmetrical package of gray matter, but two

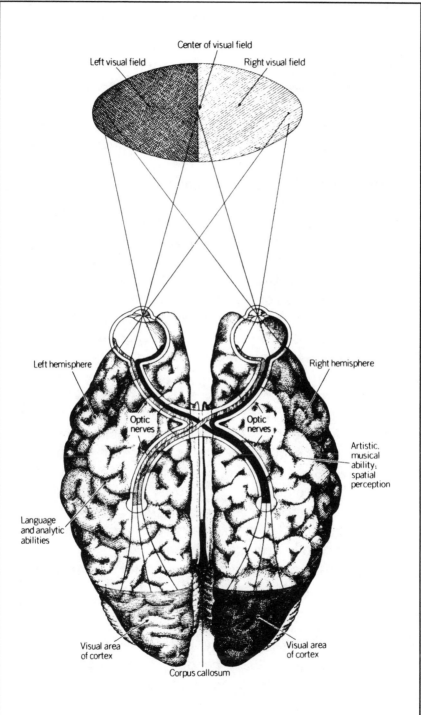

Center of visual field

Left visual field

Right visual field

Left hemisphere

Right hemisphere

Optic nerves

Optic nerves

Artistic, musical ability; spatial perception

Language and analytic abilities

Visual area of cortex

Visual area of cortex

Corpus callosum

*The two hemispheres of the brain have entirely different functions. The brain's organization ususally dictates not only which hand you prefer, but which foot, ear, and eye as well.*

"complementary brains," which work together as a team. Each hemisphere has specific tasks totally different from those of the other.

For most people, the left hemisphere of the brain is the language center and source of logical thinking. It is from the left hemisphere that most people work out math problems, memorize chemistry formulas, and learn how to spell. The right half of the brain usually controls broader concepts, such as intuitions and our reactions to the five senses. How we see forms and shapes and how we react to sounds and smells are generally controlled from the right half of the brain. The process by which we are able to grasp everything at once, with the result that we get a general impression or feeling from, say, a painting or song, is called "holistic thinking." For most people holistic thinking originates in the right half of the brain.

There is some evidence that lefties have an edge on achievements that rely on holistic concepts. One study edited by *Dr. Herron*, for example, focused on 103 students at Massachusetts College of Art and Boston University's School of Fine Arts and compared them to 87 liberal arts undergraduates. Of the art majors, 47 percent were left-handed or mixed-handed, while only 22 percent (even this is way off the population average) of the liberal arts students were.

Another report revealed that left-handed architects also seem to thrive. In a study of 405 right-handed architecture students, only 62 percent finished the course, while 73 percent of the 79 lefties completed their studies. Incidentally, in this survey, 29 percent of the faculty were left-handed. These high statistics are generally attributed to a left-hander's greater sense

of spatial relations - the same skill at visualizing geometric patterns which leads lefties to excel at chess.
In line with the brain's duality, as it were, the left hemisphere dictates the movements of the right hand and right side of the body; the right hemisphere moves the left hand, left foot, left side. If our brains and our bodies were all neat and simple, then we would find that right-handers would be the mathematicians, computer experts and scientists, while lefties would be the artists and architects, the composers, the writers -the creative geniuses.

But it doesn't work out that conveniently. *Jeannine Herron* pointed out that both hemispheres are "connected by an enormous bundle of fibers called the *corpus callosum*, which allows almost instant communication between the two brain hemispheres. The right hand has access to information in both hemispheres, as does the left."

Still, right-handers generally have their "language center" in the left hemisphere, while only six out of ten lefties process language on the left. The rest of the left-handed population uses either the right side of the brain or both sides. If a dextral person is damaged on the left side of the brain through an accident or illness, he or she usually loses the power of speech. But a sinistral, who is more likely to utilize both brain hemispheres, can often regain language skill, no matter which half of the brain is injured.

Researcher Jerre Levy of the Bio-Psychology Committee at the University of Chicago, believes that lefties who write in the upside-down fashion called "the hook" are the 60 percent with language centers in the left hemisphere, while the 40 percent who write in a mirror image of righties have language centers in the right sphere. (More about the writing problems of left-ies in the next chapter).

In an article in *Science Digest*, another researcher, psychologist Dr. Theodore Blau, observed that southpaws are likely "to be imaginative and for some peculiar reason prefer swimming underwater, much more than right-handers."

The brain organization not only dictates which hand you prefer, but also which foot, or eye, or ear. The preference, of course, doesn't actually lie in the hand or the foot or the eye or the ear. It lies in the *brain*. Although nobody ever says, "Wow, you're left-eared," this is part of the same picture as being left-handed. Lab tests, for example, reveal that left-handed people are much more perceptive of changes in musical notes.

The magazine *Scientific American* printed a study in which subjects listened to certain tonal sequences through earphones: One ear received a high tone; the other a low tone. It was reported that "right-handed subjects tended strongly to hear the high tone in their right ear and the low tone in their left ear and to maintain this percept when the earphones were reversed."

Left-handers, in contrast, "were just as likely to [hear] the high tone in their left ear as in their right." In other words, lefties tend to be ambi-aural (to coin a word) as well as ambidextrous.

## HOW MANY LEFTIES ARE THERE?

While current research puts the figure at about fifteen percent of the population, (in America that amounts to some 40 million people) some scientists think that as much as half of humanity would be left-handed if they hadn't been trained to use their right hands as children. (Interestingly, lab tests on cats and dogs show that paw preference is balanced at about 50-50. An informal survey taken by an animal lover who feeds about twenty bears at his New York state farm, however, indicates that about 90 percent of his bears are *lefties.*) The proportion of lefties to righties also varies according to the culture they live in. Clearly, there are more lefties in countries where left-handedness is accepted and fewer in countries like Africa, India, Asia, and the Arab nations, where the left hand is still believed to be the "unclean" hand.

To determine if someone is left-handed or right-handed, researchers very often use the "torque test." All you have to do is draw a circle, first with one hand and then with the other. Lefties and ambidextrals draw circles with a clockwise motion. Right-handed people usually make circles in counterclockwise style.

## DO LEFTIES HAVE MORE PHYSICAL PROBLEMS?

Although "brain damage" may be too strong a word, there is a correlation between being left-handed or ambidextrous and several physiological conditions, among them *stuttering* and *dyslexia* (reading backwards or transposing letters or numbers), which often go hand-in-hand. Dr. Bryng Bryngelson, the Minnesota researcher who studied handedness for over thirty years, found that four times as many ambidextrous people rather than

*This sketch of Alice, from Carroll's **Through The Looking Glass**, illustrates the duality, or mirror image, which Carroll often used in his stories. At upper left, Alice is shown peering into the looking glass, and at right, stepping through the looking glass.*

true righties were stutterers. One explanation he gives is that since it's more frustrating for lefties or ambidextrals to deal with tools, customs and other traditions of a right-handed world, this "confuses" the brain and leads to stammering. The situation is even worse when a child is "switched" and forced to use the right hand.

There are many documented cases of the relationship between switched hands and stuttering. As noted earlier, England's *King George VI* was switched to writing with his right hand as a child, but he always played tennis and golf skillfully with his *left* hand. Later on in life, he taped and edited his radio broadcasts to eliminate the stammered words. Another king who was switched as a child, *Louis II* of France, became known as "Louis the Stammerer".

One man who should have been a lefty and spent his life stammering because of an early switch was *Lewis Carroll*, author of *Alice's Adventures in Wonderland* and *Through the Looking Glass*. In the Alice books there is always a duality, a mirror image, which confused Carroll in his own life. Tweedledum and Tweedledee are mirror images of each other. And in *Through the Looking Glass*, everything is reversed. Alice walks *backwards* to meet the Queen; the Red Queen cries *before* she pricks her finger; the White Knight is the one who might "madly squeeze a right-hand foot into a left-hand shoe." (Lefties, who have trouble with directions and in remembering which foot is which, do this all the time).

Stuttering and dyslexia may be cause for concern, but they are not life-threatening. Several years ago, however, a book was published which literally gave lefties cause to fear for their lives. In 1992, psychologist Stanley Coren published *The Left-Hander Syndrome: The Causes and Consequences of Left-Handedness* in which he concluded that lefties die an average of nine years earlier than righties! While Coren's statement generated headlines (and probably raised the heart attack rate among southpaws), it also generated criticism from scientists. Critics pointed out that Coren's study was based on limited research of *older* lefties, many past 70. Since switching was common in the early part of the century, there were obviously not many lefties left to enjoy their old age. and participate in Coren's research. In addition, researchers found that the sample on which his conclusions were based was too small to be scientifically significant. Coren then revised his figures downward and maintained that on the average, lefties died about four or five years earlier than righties.

There is some merit to this revised figure. For example, southpaws are involved in more accidents than right-handers. One reason is that when driving a car, lefties tend to jerk the wheel counterclockwise, and therefore head *toward* the oncoming traffic they are trying to avoid. In addition, the right-handed majority designs most of the tools and equipment used in industry, and consequently, the way-things-work favors righties. When industrial accidents happen to lefties using drill presses or metal spinners or lathes, or operating bulldozers or cranes or other earth moving equipment, a causative factor might involve *where* the controls and safety switches are located. The same is true with smaller tools–hand drills, electric saws, other power tools.

In terms of illnesses, scientists have also found some correlation between lefties and alcoholism, epilepsy, psychoses, depression and other mental disorders, in addition to such learning disabilities as dyslexia. Because of a suppressed immune system, left-handers are also at higher risk for such ailments as rheumatoid arthritis, migraines and diabetes, and more vulnerable to hayfever, asthma and allergies. (When lefties are fighting an infection they should remind their doctors they may require higher doses of antibiotics to be effective).

Left-handers also have some physical problems at the earliest stages of life. Fifty-four percent of premature babies are lefties, and in cases of stressful births, more male infants are born left-handed than girls (which may tie in with the fact that more boys than girls suffer from dyslexia and stuttering).

But, but, but–there are definite pluses to being lefthanded. Lefties are over-represented in the ranks of the gifted: One study showed that over 20 percent of those who scored more than 700 on SAT's were lefties and over 20 percent of Mensa's members are left-handers. Even the right-handed Dr. Coren, whose book is not a happy read for southpaws, concludes "The implication is that left-handers are apt to be extremely dull or extremely bright." At least he got that half right!

## WHEN DO WE BECOME LEFTIES?

Although hand preference first makes its appearance when a child is about six months old, for the next two years any baby will be quite unpredictable as to which hand will dominate. Often a child will use either hand interchangeably for eating, throwing, catching, other everyday tasks. From three to six years, hand preference becomes firmly established or permanently frustrated. If a right-handed mother insists on giving her child a spoon or fork in his or her right hand, a true lefty may instead grow up to be a confused righty.

Many lefties, however, are ambidextrous to some degree, either through convenience or brain organization or social pressures, and have actually learned to make the best of both worlds.

###

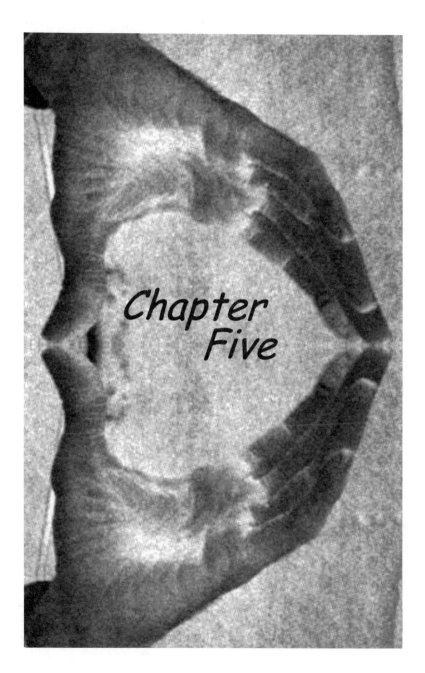

Chapter
Five

# Which Is The Right Meaning For "Left"?

Where did the word "left" and other words associated with being left-handed come from? All the world's major languages have special terms for being left-sided or left-handed...and very few of them are flattering.

## LATIN

When you think of how many languages have their origins in Latin, it's clear how far-reaching the influence of the Roman Empire was. There are two Latin word roots which have to do with lefties: the first is *laevus*, an old term for "left hand." The second is *sinister*, which really meant "the pocket side." Pockets in a toga were always on the left but this didn't come to mean "sinister' as we know it until the Romans adopted the Greek method of predicting events, called "augury."

An augur (fortune-teller) would stand in a certain direction and then predict coming wars, power struggles, or other major events. In the Greek method of augury, the fortune-tellers faced north and favored the right hand. Anything on the left therefore became sinister, ominous.

Derivatives of the Latin root *laevus* emerge in other ancient languages:

Middle and Old English:
the words are *left* or *lift*, meaning "weak or "worthless."

Old German or Dutch:
*loof, luchter, lucht, luft, leeft,* meaning "weak."

Anglo Saxon:
*lyft,* meaning "weak" or "broken."

## MODERN LANGUAGES

In Modern English, *The Oxford Dictionary* gives such definitions of left-handed as:

1. Having the left hand more serviceable than the right; using the left hand by preference.
2. (Figuratively) a. crippled, defective; b. awkward, clumsy, inept; c. characterized by underhand dealings.
3. Ambiguous, doubtful, questionable.
4. Ill-omened, sinister.

In the *American Random House Dictionary*, left-handed is defined as "rotating counterclockwise; ambiguous or doubtful as in a left-handed compliment; clumsy or awkward." In addition to "clumsy" and "awkward," *Webster's* includes the term "morganatic," used to describe the ancient custom in which a nobleman, when marrying a commoner, would give her his left hand instead of the right, therefore denying her certain legal rights.

That ominous trend prevails in other modern languages: In French, "left" is *gauche*, which also means "awkward" or "clumsy." The Portuguese word for "left," *canhoto*, translates as "weak" or "awkward." In Romany, the word for "left," *bongo*, means "crooked" or "evil." This evil definition is also seen in *Italian*, where *mancini* ("left") means "crooked" or even "maimed." In Spanish, *zurdo* not only means "left" but is sometimes also used as an equivalent for *malicioso* ("evil"). *No ser zurdo* means "to be very clever," that is, "*not* to be left-handed." In Russian, to label someone a "left-hander–*levja*–is a term of insult; in Polish, *lewo* means not quite legal, rather sneaky.

In addition to the formal meanings and interpretations for "left," "left-handed," or "left-sided," there are slang meanings that are well known. When you're not playing baseball, being "out in left field" means "completely mistaken," and "left-handed wisdom" is a collection of junk, mistakes. A "left-handed compliment" is actually an insult. A son "from the left side" is illegitimate, while getting out of bed on the wrong side (which actually means the *left* side) signals that you are in a bad mood, or that this is going to be a very bad day.

In political terms a leftist is too liberal, revolutionary...even a communist! H.L. Mencken, the American journalist who was fascinated by the meanings of words, explained the term "leftist" in his book *The American Language*. He said the word was first introduced by historian *Thomas Carlyle* in his *French Revolution*, written in 1837.

*Carlyle* described a leftist as someone who sat on the French president's *côte gauche* (left side). These included the radicals, members of the press, and revolutionaries. The aristocrats sat on the president's right, and the moderates sat directly before him.

Because of such colloquialisms, through the years left-handers have had to cope with the prevailing idea that they must be doing something wrong, certainly not "right."

There are other slang words for left-handers, some good and others bad. In the United States the term "southpaw" comes from the fact that a left-handed pitcher faces south when he or she winds up to throw the ball. Now the term is used not only for lefties in general, but also for all left-handed athletes.

Australians call lefties "molly-dookers," from *molly*, which means "a sissyish man," and *dukes*, slang for "hands." In Northern Ireland, the Protestants call their Catholic enemies "left-footers," an unflattering nickname.

"Left out" means you don't get to play, and nobody wants to eat "leftovers." When the right hand doesn't know what the left hand is doing, the implication is that the left hand must be doing something *wrong*.

On the positive side, though, there is one town in America which honors sinistrals: the township of Left Hand, West Virginia, population five hundred.

# SUPERSTITIONS, RELIGIONS, AND WIDDERSHINS

By the time of the ancient Romans, the belief that right was good and left was bad began to appear in all areas of human life from religion to superstition.

Some historians theorize that the reason for this was based on the movement of the sun. If you are in the northern hemisphere, and facing south, the sun moves from left-to-right across the horizon. Because the sun was and is one of the most important symbols of life, the left-to-right movement was considered the only correct way to go. The right hand, therefore, became associated with good and power; the left hand came to represent weakness and evil.

But this theory doesn't hold up if you think of people in the southern hemisphere. Since the sun moves from right-to-left during the day below the equator, people there would more likely favor the left hand if the sun really determined hand preference. But there is no greater preponderence of lefties south of the Equator than in the northern hemisphere.

One of the most famous sun symbols in history eventually came to signify infamy. But the swastika, so closely identified with Adolph Hitler and the Nazi party, showed up all over the world, centuries before World War II, in Egypt, Greece, South America, Mexico, Britain, Ireland, Spain, India, and North America. The hooks on a swastika follow the left-to-right direction of the sun's movement and actually represented good luck or good fortune.

There is another kind of swastika, however, that was considered a good luck sign by a left-handed sect that lived in southern India. This swastika, with a right-to-left movement, was adapted as a favorable omen by Rudyard Kipling; many of his books about India were decorated with the sign.

The idea that moving counter-clockwise was not only contrary, but downright evil is found in the Scottish con-

*Adolph Hitler used the swastika as a symbol of the Nazi party in Germany during the 1930s and early 1940s. Another version of the swastika–in the reverse direction from right-to-left was adapted as a favorable omen by Rudyard Kipling*

*The swastika (opposite page) as a symbol of good fortune appears in this Hopi Indian dance rattle.*

cept of *"widdershins"*, a derivation of the German word Wiederschein, meaning "against the sun." The Scots believed that devils and witches ran counter to the sun. So, if a person walked or ran widdershins, he or she was thought to admire the devil and perhaps even be a witch.

People were accused of witchcraft for such simple actions as walking around a barn from the right to the left instead of from left to right. At the Salem witch trials in New England in the seventeenth century, widdershin movements were used as evidence, but matters were made even worse if the accused witch was left-handed as well.

In France, several centuries earlier, *Joan of Arc* was burned as a witch; ironically she is now considered a saint in the Catholic Church. She came from the region of Lorraine, where people believed in the power of witchcraft and the devil. Sketches of the time show Joan carrying her sword in her *left* hand.

In many paintings and drawings, and even Tarot cards, the devil himself is depicted as being left-handed. A French superstition is that Satan greets witches and is greeted by them avec *le bras gauche*, "with the left arm."

This association of the left side with the devil is still recognized in as common a custom as throwing a little salt over your left shoulder–in other words, in the devil's direction–if you spill salt at the table. The origin

*In "A Kiss for the Devil," a woodcut from Guazzo's 17th century* **Compendium Maleficarum**, *Satan (depicted as a goat) is greeted by a kiss on the backside and three of his followers hold torches in their left hands.*

of this superstition is that at the Last Supper, before Jesus Christ was turned over to Pilate for his crucifixion, Judas, the apostle who betrayed Christ, spilled the salt.

According to popular Gypsy superstition, if the right palm itches, you'll get money; if the left palm itches, you're about to lose some loot.

The emphasis on left and right shows up in other religions as well. Orthodox Jews wear "phylacteries"–leather boxes containing Hebrew texts–on their left arms as a shield against evil influences. In the Talmud, the Prince of Demons is named Samael, from the Hebrew word for left side *(se 'mol)*. Michael sat on God's right and Samael on the left; when Samael was evicted from heaven, he was replaced by the angel Gabriel, which was a slight improvement when you consider that it's Gabriel's job to announce the end of the world.

*"Le Diable," carrying his sword in the left hand; one of the Tarot pack of 22 cards.*

Buddhists believe in two very important symbols: the Yang and the Yin. The Yang is active, male, represents light, life, and the right hand; the Yin is passive, female, earth, darkness, and the left hand. But when the two symbols are united in a circle, it becomes a symbol of harmony, something the Chinese call "the Tao."

# BEST FOOT FORWARD

The left foot plays its part in superstititions, too. In Roman times it was thought to be unlucky to enter a house with the left foot first. This practice was adopted by the Scots in a tradition called "first footing," which they still follow on Hogmanay (New Year's Eve). To enter a house with the left foot first would bring bad luck to the occupants for the new year ahead.

However, soldiers always march with the left foot first in a left-right, left-right pattern. One theory as to why the left-foot-first movement is preferred for marching is that the left leg is weaker, so that any injury incurred isn't as serious. Another explanation is that since the right arm holds the weapon, a left-foot-forward movement will give momentum for the right hand. (For one fifteenth century Scottish-Irish family named Kerr–which actually is Gaelic for "left"–the opposite was true. The clan had so many lefties that in 1470 they built the spiral staircases in their castles in reverse to make it easier for left-handed swordsmen to fence with their enemies.)

One left-foot supersitition is lucky for humans, unlucky for rabbits. During early days in America, a rabbit was always on hand whenever someone was executed. The animal's left hind leg was cut off and given to the executioner to protect him from misfortune. And that's how the rabbit's foot became a common good luck charm.

###

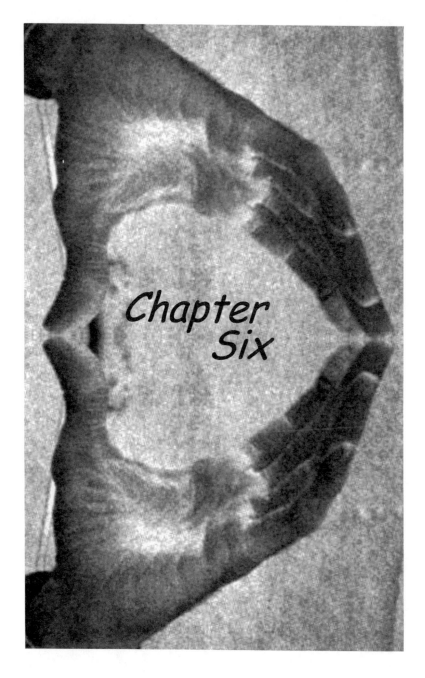

Chapter
Six

# Is It Easier To Fight Than Switch?

When you're left-handed, there are dozens of things you have to learn to do with your right hand. But the most difficult task all of us lefties face from the time we're old enough to hold a pencil is to *write* with our left hand.

I've never met a lefty who got an A in penmanship. The best I could ever manage was a C. My teachers always insisted that we slant our papers to the left, which of course is correct for righties but not for lefties. I very stubbornly would switch my paper to the right, which made it easier for me to write somewhat legibly.

About 60 percent of left-handers do slant their papers to the left, as instructed from kindergarten days, and therefore write in the upside down position known as "the hook," in which the writing is actually done from *above* the line. For those of us who slant to the right and write in the same fashion as righties (with the hand positioned *below* the line), the result can be sloppy because as we write we tend to smear the words already completed. But aside from neatness, the act of writing

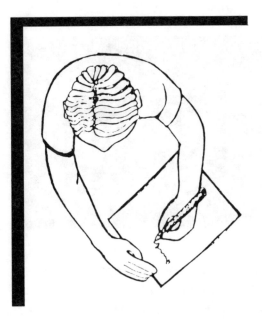

Here's how both types of lefties write:

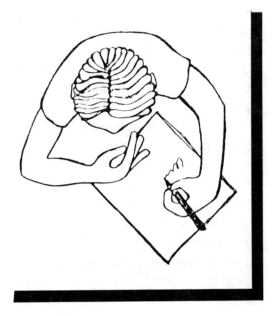

itself is physically tiring for lefties. A right-handed person, working from left to right, is actually *pulling* the pen–the pen moves naturally across the page. But lefties could well be called "pen pushers." They have to push the pen or pencil along. Because their hands get tired of pushing, they tend to write more laboriously and more carefully–and sometimes less legibly–than righties.

*Young Arkansas Attorney General Bill Clinton signs state legislation.*

It's interesting that left-handed signatures, when written carefully and painstakingly, are notoriously easy for forgers to imitate. Another factor is that lefties tend to have several variations of their signatures, depending on how tired they are or how much they've already written...or what they are writing *on* or *in*. A bound guest book, or day book, or even a check book that doesn't open flat presents a bumpy hurdle that the left hand has to cope with, which often distorts a signature or other writing

Although lefties and their left-handed writing are widely accepted today in America, England, France, Sweden, and other industrialized countries, left-handed writing is still frowned upon in such countries as Greece, Russia, and most Arab nations. Still, when children are forced to use their right hands when the preferred hand is the left, the result is often undecipherable and often gets worse, not better with age.

Although as far as we know, nobody ever forces right-handers to write with their left hands, sometimes this becomes necessary because of an injury. Historically one of the most famous switch-writers was *Lord Nelson,* the English naval hero, who lost the use of his right hand in a battle. At first his left-handed writing was awkward, clumsy, and almost illegible. But years later, after decades of practice, his left-handed script was as beautiful and precise as his original right-handed penmanship had been. One of our own war heroes, Senator *Bob Dole,* also had to learn to use his left hand for writing, but with the aid of computers, it's not necessary for him to write long compositions by hand. His signature is a quick scrawl, but so is that of most busy people required to sign their names over and over again.

Although the exact date when children were specifically taught to use their right hands for writing has not been recorded, we do know that as early as 1587 a book on handwriting in English, called *The Petie Schole,* instructed students to "hold the pen in your right hande" and that emphasis continued until the middle of our own century.

In 1950, an education teacher at Brooklyn College wrote "not to let the child get well started in left-handedness for any skill he is likely to use steadily, that is eating, writing, sewing and using household tools and equipment" beginning in nursery school. While some schools were more liberal than others in enforcing this rule, parochial schools were unremittingly strict. *Babe Ruth* provides a typical example: The nuns and priests who raised him were able to carry through on his writing–all his life he wrote right-handed–but fortunately weren't able to change the way he played baseball...he always threw and batted southpaw fashion.

Despite the stress that right is right, there was one small, but strong, group whose goal was to encourage the equal use of *both hands*, the Ambidextral Culture Society which originated in England at the turn of the last century and then spread to the United States. The movement was sparked by the ideas of one proponent, novelist Charles Reade, who, in 1878, wrote in *Harper's Weekly*

> *I believe that "THE COMING MAN" is the "EITHER-HANDED MAN"–that is to say, neither "right-handed" nor "left-handed"–but a man rescued in time from parroted mother, cuckoo nurses, and starling nursing-maids, with their pagan nursery rhymes and their pagan prejudices against the left hand.*

Given such well-promoted encouragement, an expert on handwriting, John Jackson, founded the society and published a book which included such credos as "JUSTICE AND EQUALITY FOR THE LEFT HAND!" There were many well-known supporters of the society, including Lord R.S.S. Baden-Powell, founder of the Boy Scouts (remember their left-handed shake?) and well-known painter Sir Edwin Lanseer, who also gave drawing lessons to left-handed *Queen Victoria*.

Within a decade, however, the Ambidextral Culture Society faded from public popularity, a victim no doubt of majority–right-handed–rule.

# WORD GAMES LEFTIES PLAY

While there are problems that arise from working left to right when you'd rather go the other way, there are also fascinating word games at which southpaws seem to excel. This peculiar skill may be a result of the confusion that sometimes arises because lefties are more likely to process information from both sides of the brain. One of these games is called a *spoonerism*, named after *Dr. Spooner* of Oxford University. Dr. Spooner not only mixed up *b's* and *p's* and *6's* and *9's*, but he frequently transposed letters and words so that

*Conquering Kings* became *Kingering Congs*

*Let us have flags hung from the window in his honor*
became
*Let us have hags flung from the window in his honor*

*Spooner's* research showed that lefties are much more likely than righties to mix up such sentences. Most sinistrals are also fascinated by palindromes, phrases or sentences that can be read backwards or forwards. Some classic examples:
  *Draw pupil's lip upward.* Read that from right to left and you'll see it says exactly the same thing.
  Another is:
  *A man, a plan, a canal-panama!*
  One of my all-time favorite palindromes is one that might have been said by the first man to his mate:
  *"Madam, I'm Adam."*
  Her reply, of course, was, *"Eve."*

# LEFTIES ARE FLEXIBLE

Almost from the time we learn to use our hands to perform tasks, lefties also learn how to adjust. Eating is one of the most common examples of this flexibility. Most lefties use a knife with their right hand and the fork with their left...they don't bother switching the fork to their other hand as most righties do. Actually, this is a much more graceful method of eating than the constant switching that goes on when right-handers "enjoy" a meal. It's also the common practice–no matter which is the preferred hand–in Europe. But when a lefty is using a knife alone–let's say when cutting cheese or peeling a piece of fruit–usually the knife is held firmly in the *left hand.*

One modern convenience that seems to favor the left is the telephone. Although it was designed for dialing and depositing coins with the right hand, the receiver is usually held to the left ear, a lefty's "better" ear. The down side, however, is that when lefties are holding the phone to the left ear with the left hand and need to write a message, the phone has to be scrunched between the ear and the shoulder to leave the writing hand free. If you try to use your right ear and right hand, the wire may get in the way.

So, lefties learn to perform many acts, chores, or tasks ambidextrously: They learn to turn right to open doors, lock windows, close suitcases, use keys, wind clocks, sharpen pencils, turn on the hot water, start a car, use an adding machine or calculator, work a vacuum clearner, or play a record. If you're cooking you have to be *adroit* (literally, graceful with the right hand) at tilting some appliances with the right hand because the pouring lip is set up for dextrals. Of course you can also tip it *backwards* with your left.

Everything of importance in most cars is on the right: the ignition switch, the gear shift, the radio or tape deck, the lighter, the ashtray. The accelerator and brake, of course, are worked with the right foot, even though you, lefty, are probably left-footed.

Word processers, and computers are geared for right-handers, although the "Querty keyboard"–so-called for the first six letters underneath the numbers –was designed specifically to slow-down *right-handed typists!* When the first typewriters were designed over a century ago, the keys would jam if the operater typed too fast. So the "qwerty" arrangement, as well as the rest of the keyboard placed the keys in awkward positions for right-handers. (Although the "Dvorak keyboard" was created to correct this, the new placement was never widely accepted, a fate similar to the metric system of measurement) For years, therefore, most of the speed-typing contests were won by left-handers.

That advantage changed, however, with the design of word processors and computers, in which the most significant keys are on the right, including the numerical keyboard, the enter and backspace keys, the period, comma, and those essential keys that let you delete, insert, page up, page down, go home...or end.

We mentioned the righty-friendly power tools and industrial equipment earlier. But even the sportier side of life is right angled–think of the reels on fishing rods; also some rifles and pistols are more easily operated with the right hand. Field hockey sticks are not usually made for lefties, although ice hockey sticks are. It's

*Lefty Charlie Chaplin, who once had great ambitions to be
a concert violinist, is shown here in the movie **The
Vagabond**, playing the violin widdershins.*

difficult for a left-hander to play polo because of the direction of play and the crucial importance of the right of way. (*Prince Charles* plays polo right-handed.)

Making music generally favors righties, too, although the piano and such instruments as the clarinet or saxophone, must be played with both hands (there is no such thing as a left-handed saxophone) stringed instruments–the guitar, bass guitar, violin, banjo, mandolin–are all stringed for right-hand play. *Charlie Chaplin*, who composed most of the music for his films, wrote in *My Autobiography*: "Since the age of sixteen I had practiced from four to six hours a day in my bedroom...as I played left-handed, my violin was strung left-handed with the bass bar and sounding post reversed. I had great ambitions to be a concert artist...but as time went by I realized I could not achieve excellence, so I gave it up." In Chaplin's 1952 classic film *Limelight*, the actor is featured playing his violin "widdershins," but many amateur musicians learn to play string instruments right-handed. (Actor *Keanu Reeves*, who would rather be a successful rock star than a film star, plays his bass as a righty).

There are also many manual projects that are difficult for lefties to learn. Knitting, crocheting and embroidery, for example, all pose problems, because most

KISS ME, I'M LEFT-HANDED!

instruction booklets are written for right-handers. (But see the directory at the end of this book for southpaw sources).

# RIGHT ON FOR LEFTIES

We lefties have come a long way in the years since I was a child. Today, if you choose to write with your left hand, in most schools you'll be encouraged, not switched. Left-handed scissors are common in kindergarten - while I never owned one and have always cut right-handed. When I went to college, all the classroom seats with their mini "desks" were for righties; now, most class-rooms include a percentage of left-handed chairs. At a dinner party or restaurant, if you request the outside left-hand place setting, nobody raises a curious eyebrow. The hostess or your dinner partners realize this makes dining easier for everybody, not just you–no banging el-bows with the person next to you.

Not only is society generally more understanding, but we do have our champions, too. In 1975, *Dean Campbell* and his late wife, *Marjorie*, founded Lefthanders International, for what had been until then a fairly silent minority. Today, the Topeka, Kansas-based organization publishes a bi-monthly magazine, an annual catalogue, the Lefthander of the Year Award, and In-ternational Lefthanders Day, held every August 13th-the first one in 1975 fell on a Friday and was specifi-cally chosen to spoof the superstitions associated with lefties.

# What's Left!

If the Right side of the body is controlled by the Left side of the brain, & the Left side of the body is controlled by the Right side of the brain, then LEFT HANDED people are the only ones in their RIGHT MINDS!!

*Campbell* strongly upholds his "Bill of Lefts" which includes the credo "Left-handers shall be entitled to offer their dominant hand in a handshake, salute or oath." This very vocal lefty says "If the right side of the body is controlled by the left side of the brain and vice versa, then we left-handed people are the only ones in our right mind."

Sometimes, however, our minds get muddled by the plethora of "the right stuff." Fortunately, today there are good sources and products which offer "the left stuff" to help us function in a right-handed world. You can buy a left-handed iron or scissors in most hardware stores. You can adapt the mouse on your computer to use with your left hand. There are books that teach you how to do needlepoint or play golf left-handed, and stores or mail-order catalogues that provide dozens of items from left-handed bowling gloves to left-handed grapefruit knives. Some of the most unusual tools and equipment include:

- A device to attach to the gear shift of a car so you can shift with your left hand.
- A left-foot accelerator.
- A left-handed ruler with numbers beginning at the right.
- A thermometer you can read while holding it in your left hand.
- Left-handed power tools- drills, saws, screwdrivers.
- Left-handed playing cards with numbers in all four corners for easier fanning.
- Archery sets strung for lefties.
- All types of sports equipment, even a boomerang.

- Left-handed diaper pins.
- Left-handed can openers, mixing tools, vegetable parers, ice cream scoops.
- Calligraphy sets with nibs angled for southpaws.
- Cameras with shutters on the left.
- Left-handed corkscrews.
- Swiss Army knives with lefty-geared gadgets.
- Items that celebrate your sinistral status from T-shirts to bumper stickers.

Among my favorite purchases is a T-shirt imprinted "Lefties of the World Unite," and a giant button that reads "Kiss Me, I'm Left-Handed."

I've always liked being left-handed; it made me feel different and special. And I've found that left-handed people have a kindred spirit of affection and appreciation for other lefties. It's as if we belong to our own unique club. You don't have to pay any dues to belong to this club, and you don't even have to learn the "Bill of Lefts." But you do share membership with some world-famous, very talented men and women. To be a member in good standing, all you have to do is proudly use your good *left hand!*

###

# WHAT'S LEFT?

## Shops and Sources for Southpaws

## United States:

### *Lefthanders International, Inc.*

Dean R. Campbell, founder of the international club and publisher of the bi-monthly Lefthander magazine; one-year subscription, $15.00; two years, $28.00.(Canada and Mexico, add $6.00 per year for postage; all other countries, add $18.00).

Kim Kipers and Carol Riddle, Lefthanders International mail order catalogue, $2.00

P.O. Box 8249

Topeka, Kansas 66608

Magazine: (913) 234-2177

Catalogue: (800) 203-2177

### *Left-Handed Complement*

Marcy Lewinstein

241 Perkins Street, Suite I-302

Boston, Massachusetts 02130

1-800-676-5338

Since 1976; free mail order catalogue of over 100 items (send stamped, self-addressed #10 envelope).

# WHAT'S LEFT?

## Left Hand World, Inc.
Karen H. Carlisle
Pier 39
P.O. Box 330128
San Francisco, California 94133-0128
(415) 433-3547

## Lefty's Corner
Dale Hersh
P.O. Box 615
Clarke's Summit, Pennsylvania 18411
(717) 586-5338
   Mail order catalogue with over 100 items, $2.00
   (refundable with first order)

## Lefty/Portside
Diana Ryan
920 W. Olympia Street
Hernando, Florida 34442
(800) 245-5338
   Mail order catalogue with over 125 items.

## The Southpaw Shop
Mary and T.C. Coley, Sr.
849 W. Harbor Drive, Suite "B"
San Diego, California 92101
(619) 239-1731
   Mail order catalogue available for $1.00; write to
   P.O. Box 2870, San Diego, CA 92112.

# WHAT'S LEFT?

*Woodpecker Shop*
Luz Cordero
10034 Spanish Isle Boulevard, Bay C15
Boca Raton, Florida 33498
(407) 451-9213
   Manufacturers of left-hand wooden products.

## England:

*Anything Left-handed Limited*
Keith Molsen
57 Brewer Street
London, England W1R-3FB

# ILLUSTRATIONS

# ILLUSTRATIONS

# ABOUT THE AUTHOR

In 1980, Rae Lindsay wrote *The Left-Handed Book* for her southpaw son, Rob, who was just beginning to experience the joys...and woes...of being left-handed. Sixteen years later, he's grown-up and so has her new take on the sinistral side of life. *Left is Right: The Survival Guide for Living Lefty in a Right-Handed World* is Rae's nineteenth non-

Photo Credit: Rob Lindsay

fiction book. Other titles include *The Presidents' First Ladies, Alone and Surviving, How To Look As Young As You Feel, The Pursuit of Youth, and Sleep and Dreams.*

In the past few years, between books, Rae Lindsay frequently travels to the "left coast," to visit her right-handed children, Maria in Santa Monica, and Alex, in San Francisco.